MAKING EMMIE SMILE

WALDORF PUBLISHING

Written By

Ellen Weisberg and Ken Yoffe

EX LIBRIS

CARVER

Published by Waldorf Publishing
2140 Hall Johnson Road
#102-345
Grapevine, Texas 76051
www.WaldorfPublishing.com

Making Emmie Smile

ISBN: 9781643166193

Library of Congress Control Number: 2018943979

Copyright © 2019

As a baby, Emmie wouldn't
smile...

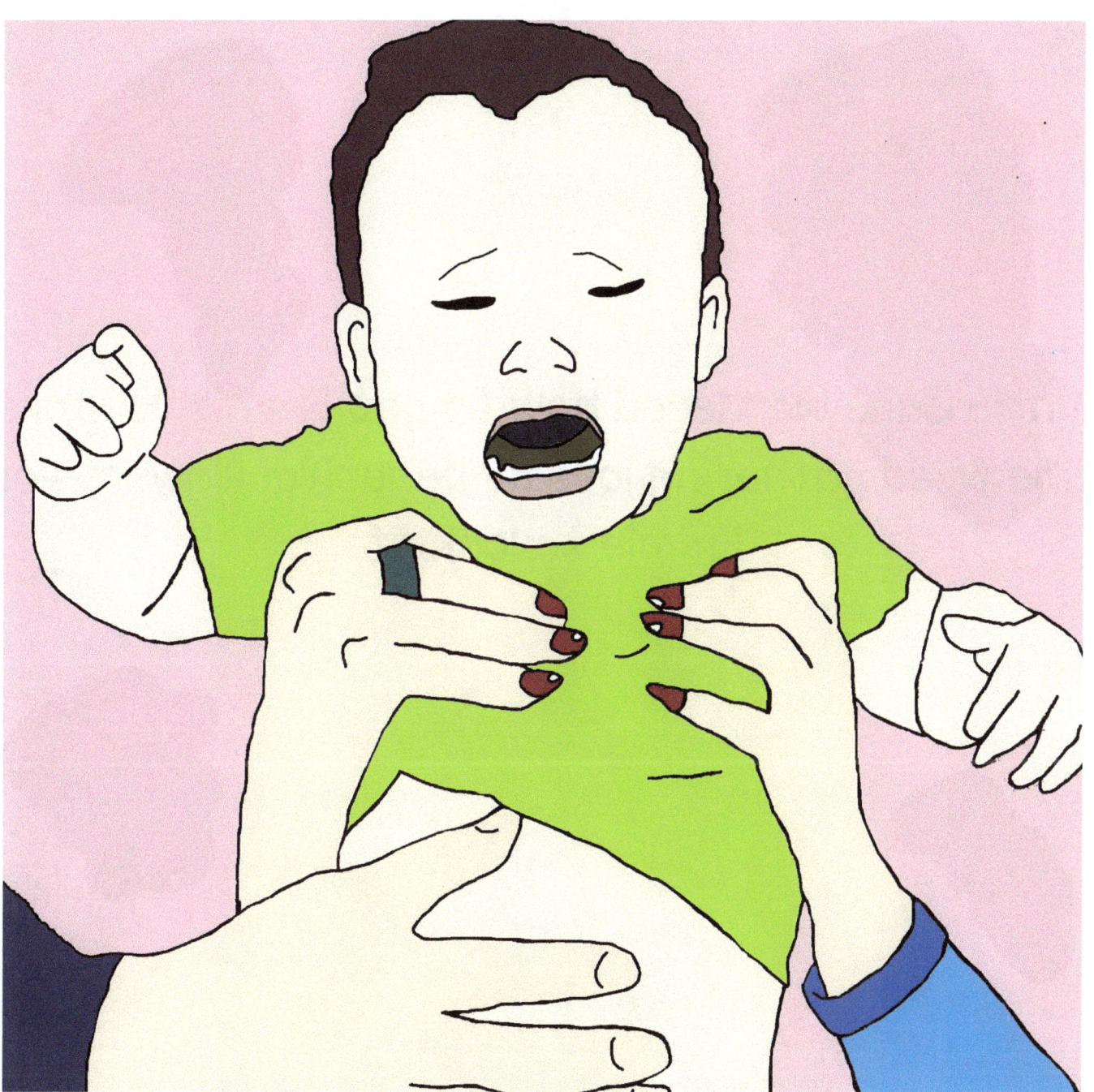

Auntie Jane wondered how to get Emmie to smile. She tried gathering lots of beautiful flowers for Emmie to look at.

It didn't work...

As Emmie grew, she still wouldn't smile.

Cousin Frank wondered how to get Emmie to smile. He tried making silly faces with his friends.

It didn´t work...

As Emmie grew, she still wouldn´t smile.

Great Grandma Mae wondered how to get Emmie to smile.
She tried finding plenty of delicious foods for Emmie to eat.

It didn't work...

As Emmie grew, she still wouldn't smile.

Nana Sheila and Poppy Joe wondered how to get Emmie to smile. They tried giving her lots of toys.

It didn't work...

As Emmie grew, she still wouldn't smile.

Then Nana Sheila had an idea. She tried tickling Emmie.

It worked!

The tickling formed a smile on Emmie's face that lasted and lasted.

The most treasured gift that we can give people is often one that we can't see.

But they can.

CPSIA information can be obtained
at www.ICGtesting.com
Printed in the USA
BVHW011109010821
613366BV00010B/649